FANCIFUL FINDINGS

DIY Jewelry

Bits and pieces that catch your fancy are fun to use in crafting jewelry.
Get inspired with these necklaces, bracelets, and more from Holly Witt-Allen.

2

4

5

6

8

10

12

14

16

19

22

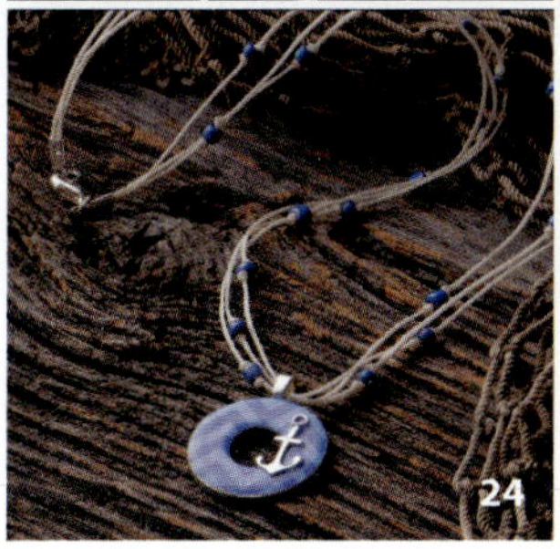
24

26

28

LEISURE ARTS, INC. • Maumelle, Arkansas

WATCH FOB NECKLACE & EARRINGS

SHOPPING LIST

- ☐ old pocket watch frame
- ☐ 2 5mm x 8 mm aqua rondelle beads
- ☐ 2 10mm aqua beads
- ☐ 2 10mm coconut spacer beads
- ☐ 9mm antique copper jump ring
- ☐ 2 4mm antique copper jump rings
- ☐ 2 antique copper ear wires
- ☐ 2 antique copper fold-over cord ends
- ☐ antique copper lobster clasp
- ☐ 18-gauge antique copper wire
- ☐ 24" length of aqua suede lacing
- ☐ 2 1/2" silver hex nuts
- ☐ 2 3/8" silver hex nuts
- ☐ 2 5/8" antique brass gears
- ☐ 3/4" brass gear
- ☐ white cardstock scrap
- ☐ Tim Holtz® Idea-ology™ game spinner with brad
- ☐ Tim Holtz® Stampers Anonymous "Time" clock and word stamps
- ☐ black archival ink pad
- ☐ Tim Holtz® Distress Inks (Mowed Lawn, Peacock Feathers, Squeezed Lemonade, and Vintage Photo)
- ☐ Ranger® mini ink blending tool and sponge applicators
- ☐ craft glue
- ☐ découpage glue
- ☐ small paintbrush
- ☐ dimensional foam stickers
- ☐ wax paper
- ☐ 1/16" hole punch
- ☐ round-nose pliers
- ☐ chain-nose pliers (2 pair)
- ☐ wire cutters

Be sure to read the General Instructions *on pages 30-32* *before making your project.*

To make each Earring:

1. Cut a 3" wire length and make a loop at one end. String the beads, nuts, and spacer bead on the wire. Make a wrapped loop attaching the earring to an ear wire.
2. Attach a 5/8" gear to the earring bottom.

To make the Necklace:

Necklace Finished Length: About 24", excluding pendant

1. Cut a cardstock circle that will fit in the watch frame.
2. Working on wax paper, dab the blending tool on the Peacock Feathers ink pad 2-3 times. Starting off the cardstock circle and moving the blending tool in a circular motion, lightly touch the outer edges of the cardstock and work inward. Add touches of Mowed Lawn and Squeezed Lemonade near the center. Stamp the words and clock with the black ink. Add some "antiquing" to the outer edges with the Vintage Photo. Without re-inking your blending tool, dab some ink over the whole circle to lightly age it. Seal with a thin coat of découpage glue.
3. Punch a hole near the circle center and attach the 3/4" gear and spinner with the brad.

4. Adhere the circle in the watch frame with the dimensional stickers.
5. Fold the suede lacing in half and loop it through the watch frame with a lark's head knot *(Fig. 1)*. Attach a fold-over cord end to each suede lacing end.

Fig. 1

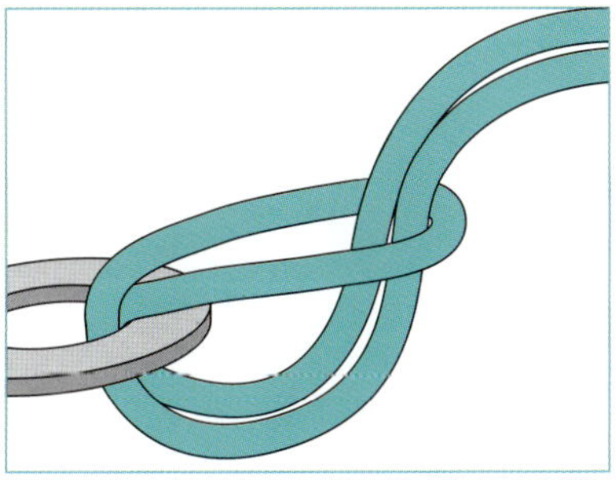

6. Attach the 9mm jump ring to one cord end. Attach a 4mm jump ring to the remaining cord end. Use the remaining 4mm jump ring to attach the clasp to the first 4mm jump ring.

BUTTERFLY BOTTLE CAP NECKLACE

SHOPPING LIST

- ☐ black bottle cap
- ☐ butterfly charm
- ☐ rhinestone
- ☐ small button
- ☐ small antique brass key
- ☐ 7mm antique copper jump ring
- ☐ 2 5mm antique brass jump rings
- ☐ 4mm antique brass jump ring
- ☐ 20" black ball chain necklace
- ☐ 2" length of antique brass small link chain
- ☐ 24-gauge antique brass wire
- ☐ scrap of cardstock with script writing
- ☐ water-based dimensional adhesive (we used Judikins Diamond Glaze™)
- ☐ small paintbrush
- ☐ fine metal file
- ☐ 1/8" dia. metal hole punch
- ☐ round-nose pliers
- ☐ chain-nose pliers (2 pair)
- ☐ wire cutters

Be sure to read the General Instructions on pages 30-32 before making your project.

To make the Necklace:

Necklace Finished Length: About 20", excluding pendant

1. Tear a circle of the script cardstock to fit on the bottle cap. Adhere the circle to the bottle cap with a thin layer of dimensional adhesive. Allow to dry.
2. Cut the loop off the butterfly charm and lightly file the cut ends until smooth.
3. Cover the surface of the cardstock with dimensional adhesive. Place the butterfly charm and the rhinestone in the adhesive. Apply a bit more adhesive along the edges of the butterfly. Allow to dry completely.
4. Use the 4mm jump ring to attach the key to a 1/2" length of small link chain. Use the 24-gauge wire to make a wrapped loop to attach the button to a 1" length of small link chain.
5. Punch a hole at the top edge and the bottom edge of the bottle cap. Attach a 5mm jump ring to the bottle cap bottom hole. Attach the remaining 5mm jump ring to the first jump ring, threading the free ends of the key and button chains on the jump ring before closing it.
6. Attach the 7mm jump ring to the bottle cap top and thread onto the ball chain necklace.

POP TOP BRACELET

SHOPPING LIST

- ☐ 6-10 soda pop can tabs
- ☐ 44-52 7mm silver jump rings
- ☐ large silver swivel clasp
- ☐ 3/4" hinge
- ☐ 5/8" silver washer
- ☐ 3/8" silver hex nut
- ☐ Vintaj® Patina™ For All Metals (Victorian Gold)
- ☐ Vintaj® Glaze Metal Sealer
- ☐ small paintbrush
- ☐ chain-nose pliers (2 pair)

Be sure to read the General Instructions on pages 30-32 before making your project.

To make the Bracelet:

1. Measure the clasp; add 1". Subtract this measurement from the desired bracelet length.
2. Arrange 3-5 tabs, the hinge, and 3-5 tabs on your work surface. Check the length. Add or remove tabs from either side until the length is as close as possible to the measurement determined in Step 1.
3. Follow the manufacturer's instructions to paint half the tabs, the hinge, and the washer gold. Seal all the tabs, hinge, washer, and hex nut with the metal sealer; allow to dry.
4. Arrange the tabs, alternating the gold and silver tabs, with the hinge in the center. Join the pieces with 2 jump rings at the top and two jump rings at the bottom. Add 2 jump rings each to the tops and bottoms of the tabs on the ends.
5. Use a jump ring to attach the swivel clasp to the four jump rings on one bracelet end.
6. Use a jump ring to attach the washer to the four jump rings on the opposite bracelet end. Attach the hex nut to the washer with two joined jump rings.

GEAR & NUT NECKLACE, EARRINGS & RING

SHOPPING LIST

- ☐ 8 1/2" copper spacer beads
- ☐ 3 1/2" silver spacer beads
- ☐ 3 10mm copper faceted oval beads
- ☐ 3 10mm antique brass faceted oval beads
- ☐ 6 8mm silver daisy spacer beads
- ☐ 3 6mm antique copper beads
- ☐ 5 6mm silver beads
- ☐ 16 metallic gold seed beads
- ☐ 10mm silver jump ring
- ☐ small silver swivel clasp
- ☐ 2 silver ear wires
- ☐ brown wax linen cord
- ☐ 20-gauge silver wire
- ☐ 8 3/8" silver hex nuts
- ☐ 5/16" silver hex nut
- ☐ 3 5/8" brass gears
- ☐ 3/4" brass gear
- ☐ 3 1/2" silver washers
- ☐ Vintaj® Glaze Metal Sealer
- ☐ craft glue
- ☐ straight pin
- ☐ ring mandrel
- ☐ chain-nose pliers
- ☐ wire cutters
- ☐ bead tray (optional)

Be sure to read the General Instructions on pages 30-32 before making your project.

To make each Earring:

1. Seal a 3/8" hex nut with the metal sealer; allow to dry.
2. Slide an ear wire to the center of a 9" cord length. Leaving about 1/4", tie an overhand knot.
3. Stack the sealed nut on a copper spacer bead. Criss-cross the cord through the stacked pieces and tie an overhand knot next to the spacer bead.
4. Thread 3 seed beads on each cord end. Tie an overhand knot next to the last bead and trim each cord end.

To make the Ring:

1. Seal the 5/16" hex nut with the metal sealer; allow to dry.
2. Determine your ring size by sliding a ring that fits on the mandrel and noting the size. You will wrap the wire around the mandrel at the next larger size.
3. Cut a 20" wire length. Starting in the middle of the wire, wrap each wire end around the mandrel for a total of 6 wraps (at the larger size determined in Step 1).
4. Keeping the wires together, slide a 5/8" gear and the sealed nut on the wire ends.
5. Bend the wire back down toward the ring. Remove the ring from the mandrel and wrap the ends around the ring 3-4 times. Trim the excess wire and pinch the ends in with the chain-nose pliers.

To make the Necklace:

Necklace Finished Length: About 19"

1. Seal the remaining nuts and washers with the metal sealer; allow to dry.
2. Slide the clasp to the center of a 94" cord length. Tie an overhand knot to secure.
3. Using a bead tray or towel placed in a baking sheet, lay out the remaining beads (starting and ending with a silver bead), nuts, washers, and gears as desired, stacking the nuts and daisy spacer beads on the copper and silver spacer beads and the washers.

4. Thread the first bead on the cord and tie an overhand knot right next to the bead. Continue adding the beads, nuts, and gears, tying an overhand knot after you add each element. Criss-cross the cord through the stacked pieces and the gears. If both cord ends will not fit through a bead's hole, just let one cord lie against the bead back; tie the overhand knot with both cords held together.
5. Once all the beads, gears, and stacked elements have been added to the necklace, slide the 10mm jump ring on the cords. Tie a few overhand knots to secure. Firmly press the knots together. Thread 2 seed beads on each cord end. Tie an overhand knot next to the last bead and trim each cord end.

HINGE NECKLACE & EARRINGS

SHOPPING LIST

- ☐ 3 3/4" brass hinges
- ☐ 4 10 mm faceted copper oval beads
- ☐ 6 10mm faceted brass oval beads
- ☐ 4 5mm silver cube beads
- ☐ 2 6mm silver beads
- ☐ 2 1/2" copper spacer beads
- ☐ 2 14mm antique copper hoops
- ☐ 2 7mm silver jump rings
- ☐ 2 4mm antique brass jump rings
- ☐ 12 silver eye pins
- ☐ 2 silver ear wires
- ☐ antique brass square toggle clasp
- ☐ 21" length of antique brass chain
- ☐ brown wax linen cord
- ☐ Vintaj® Glaze Metal Sealer
- ☐ 2 3/8" silver hex nuts
- ☐ straight pin
- ☐ round-nose pliers
- ☐ chain-nose pliers (2 pair)
- ☐ wire cutters

Be sure to read the General Instructions on pages 30-32 before making your project.

To make each Earring:

1. Seal the hex nuts with the metal sealer; allow to dry.
2. Stack a nut on a copper spacer bead. Criss-cross an 8" cord length though the stacked pieces. Lay the spacer bead and nut flat and pull the cord ends in opposite directions to "lock" the nut to the spacer bead. Tie an overhand knot close to the spacer bead.
3. Thread a silver bead onto both cord ends and tie an overhand knot close to the silver bead. Thread a brass oval bead on one cord. Letting the remaining cord run along the back of the bead, tie a few overhand knots with both cords close to the oval bead.
4. Use the chain-nose pliers to open the loop on an ear wire. Slip the loop through the knot and close. Trim the excess cord and squeeze the knots together.

To make the Necklace:

Necklace Finished Length: About 19"

1. Seal the hinges with the metal sealer; allow to dry.
2. Use the 7mm jump rings to connect the 3 hinges, connecting through the top holes only.
3. Make 4 copper oval bead connectors, 4 silver cube bead connectors, and 4 brass oval bead connectors.
4. Referring to the photo for placement, open the loops and join the connectors to the hinges and the 14mm hoops.
5. Cut two 10 1/2" chain lengths. Thread one length through a 14mm hoop and use a 4mm jump ring to join both chain ends to a clasp piece. Repeat with the remaining chain length and clasp piece on the other side of the necklace.

KEY FOB

SHOPPING LIST

- ☐ wine cork
- ☐ 14mm purple bead
- ☐ 5mm rhinestone rondelle bead
- ☐ clear seed bead
- ☐ 18-gauge silver wire
- ☐ silver lanyard hook
- ☐ 24mm silver split ring
- ☐ muslin scrap
- ☐ white paper
- ☐ 3" square of cardboard
- ☐ assorted rubber stamps (we used a butterfly, script writing, and words)
- ☐ black permanent ink pad
- ☐ an old book (to tear from)
- ☐ embroidery floss (2 colors)
- ☐ white acrylic paint
- ☐ découpage glue
- ☐ small paintbrush
- ☐ awl
- ☐ round-nose pliers
- ☐ chain-nose pliers (2 pair)
- ☐ wire cutters

Be sure to read the General Instructions on pages 30-32 before making your project.

To make the Key Fob:

1. Cut a piece of muslin that is the height of the cork and wraps around the cork with a slight overlap. Pull a few threads to fray the top and bottom edges.
2. Lightly paint the muslin piece with the white paint (thin the paint down slightly with just a bit of water). Do not saturate the muslin with paint. Allow the paint to dry.
3. Tear a few phrases/sentences from the book and use the découpage glue to adhere the paper to the muslin piece, applying the paper at different angles. Once dry, lightly brush the thinned white paint over a few of the torn paper pieces. Allow to dry.
4. Stamp the script writing over a few of the torn paper pieces. Stamp words on plain white paper; tear out the words and use découpage glue to adhere them to the muslin. Allow to dry.
5. Lightly brush the thinned white paint over the muslin center and allow to dry. Stamp a butterfly in this area.
6. Use the découpage glue to adhere the muslin piece to the cork. Allow to dry. Brush a final coat of the découpage glue over the entire cork to seal. Allow to dry thoroughly.
7. To make the tassel, hold both floss colors together and wrap the floss around the cardboard square 12 times, starting and ending at the bottom. Trim the excess floss. Slide the tassel off the cardboard. Tie a 12" floss length around the tassel top about $^{3}/_{8}$" from the top loop; knot securely and hide the knot in the tassel. Cut the bottom loops open.
8. Push the awl all the way through the cork center, creating a tunnel for the wire.
9. Cut an 8" wire length. Make a wrapped loop on one end, slipping the tassel into the loop before wrapping. Starting at the bottom, slide the wire through the cork and thread the beads on the wire at the top. Make a large wrapped loop at the top.
10. Use the lanyard hook to attach the split ring to the loop at the top of the key fob.

LIFE

KEY CHARM NECKLACE & EARRINGS

SHOPPING LIST

- ☐ 7 5mm teal rondelle beads
- ☐ 24" length of suede lace cord
- ☐ 8 1/2" length of antique silver large link chain, plus 4 links of chain for earrings
- ☐ 5 brass ball head pins
- ☐ 10mm antique silver jump ring
- ☐ 9 7mm antique brass jump rings
- ☐ 3 6mm antique brass jump rings
- ☐ 2 small keyhole charms
- ☐ antique brass swivel clasp
- ☐ 2 antique silver ear wires
- ☐ antique brass fold-over cord end
- ☐ 3 3/8" silver hex nuts
- ☐ 5/8" brass gear
- ☐ 5 Tim Holtz® Idea-ology™ Charms (typewriter keys, a key, a muse token, and a philosophy tag)
- ☐ Vintaj® Glaze Metal Sealer
- ☐ craft glue
- ☐ round-nose pliers
- ☐ chain-nose pliers (2 pair)
- ☐ wire cutters

Be sure to read the General Instructions on pages 30-32 before making your project.

To make each Earring:

1. Use a 6mm jump ring to attach 2 chain links to a keyhole charm. Attach the keyhole charm to an ear wire.
2. Thread 2 teal rondelle beads on a head pin. Make a wrapped bead dangle, attaching the head pin to the end of the chain links.

To make the Necklace:

Necklace Finished Length: About 21", excluding charms

1. Seal the hex nuts with the metal sealer; allow to dry.
2. Arrange the charms, gear and hex nuts along the chain length. Use the 7mm jump rings to attach the charms, gear, and nuts to the chain, adding 3 wrapped bead dangles (use a head pin and teal rondelle bead for each) as desired.
3. Fold the suede cord in half and loop it through the swivel clasp with a lark's head knot *(Fig. 1)*. Attach a fold-over cord end to the ends of the suede cord.

Fig. 1

4. Use the remaining 6mm jump ring to join one chain end to the cord end. Attach the 10mm jump ring to the remaining chain end.

JOURNEY
2167
JOURNEY

HEX NUT WRAP BRACELET

SHOPPING LIST

- ☐ 5-7 4mm black rondelle beads
- ☐ small teal, orange, and purple beads for dangles
- ☐ 1 3/4" length of antique silver large link chain
- ☐ white wax linen cord
- ☐ 3 silver headpins
- ☐ antique silver lobster clasp
- ☐ 2 6mm antique silver jump rings
- ☐ 3/8" silver hex nuts (use a multiple of 3; we used 18)
- ☐ Vintaj® Patina™ For All Metals (Verdigris, Carnelian, and Amethyst)
- ☐ Vintaj® Glaze Metal Sealer
- ☐ small paintbrush
- ☐ straight pin
- ☐ round-nose pliers
- ☐ chain-nose pliers (2 pair)
- ☐ wire cutters
- ☐ bead tray (optional)

Be sure to read the General Instructions on pages 30-32 before making your project.

To make the Bracelet:

1. Follow the manufacturer's instructions to paint hex nuts verdigris, carnelian, and amethyst, painting in color groups of 3; seal the hex nuts and allow to dry.
2. This bracelet wraps around the wrist two times. Measure your wrist and multiply by 2.
3. Attach a 6mm jump ring to the clasp. Cut a length of wax cord that is 4 times the desired finished length of your bracelet plus 18". Slide the jump ring/clasp to the center of the cord and tie an overhand knot right below the jump ring.
4. Using a bead tray or a towel placed in a baking sheet, lay the nuts and beads in the following order:
   - 3 verdigris nuts, black rondelle bead
   - 3 amethyst nuts, black rondelle bead
   - 3 carnelian nuts, black rondelle bead

   Repeat this sequence to the length determined in Step 2 (or as close as possible), leaving off the black rondelle bead at the end.
5. Criss-cross the cord through the first verdigris nut and tie an overhand knot with both cords right under the nut. Repeat to add the next 2 nuts. Thread the black bead on one cord and tie an overhand knot with both cords right under the bead.
6. Repeat Step 5 until you've used all the nuts and beads laid out in Step 4.
7. Thread the remaining jump ring on the cord end and tie an overhand knot next to the last nut or bead. Tie a few tight knots and trim the excess cord. Press the knots together to seal them.
8. Attach the chain to the jump ring. Thread the teal bead onto a head pin. Make a wrapped bead dangle, attaching the head pin to the free end of the chain. Repeat to make an orange and an amethyst wrapped bead dangle.

argus
Seventy-five
ARGUS
75mm.
LUMAR

RED LEATHER NECKLACE, BRACELET & RING

SHOPPING LIST

- ☐ old "leather" purse (with flat handle for the bracelet)
- ☐ 7 assorted beads
- ☐ clear shank-style button
- ☐ chandelier glass piece with holes on 2 opposite ends
- ☐ 19" length of 2mm imitation leather black cord
- ☐ Tim Holtz® Idea-ology™ typewriter key and antique brass key charms
- ☐ 10mm antique silver jump ring
- ☐ 2 7mm antique copper jump rings
- ☐ 3 7mm silver jump rings
- ☐ 3 4mm silver jump rings
- ☐ 2 4mm antique brass jump rings
- ☐ 2 antique copper fold-over cord ends
- ☐ 2 silver metal ribbon crimp ends (the width of purse handle)
- ☐ silver ball head pin
- ☐ silver lobster clasp
- ☐ antique brass lobster clasp
- ☐ 20-gauge wire
- ☐ hand sewing needle and sewing thread to match purse handle
- ☐ lightweight cardboard scrap
- ☐ craft glue
- ☐ ring mandrel
- ☐ $^{1}/_{16}$" hole punch
- ☐ round-nose pliers
- ☐ chain-nose pliers (2 pair)
- ☐ wire cutters

Be sure to read the General Instructions on pages 30-32 before making your project.

To make the Necklace:

Necklace Finished Length: About 19", excluding pendant

1. For the pendant, cut a 1" square of cardboard. Cut a 2" square of the purse "leather." Center and glue the cardboard square on the wrong side of the leather square; let dry and trim the excess. Glue another 2" leather square to the remaining side of the cardboard; place under a heavy book while it drys to prevent curling. Trim the excess.
2. Punch a hole near the center top and center bottom of the pendant. Use the 10mm jump ring to attach the typewriter key to the pendant at the top. Use a 7mm antique copper jump ring to attach the key charm to the pendant at the bottom.
3. Attach a fold-over cord end to each end of the black cord.
4. Use a 4mm jump ring to attach the remaining 7mm antique copper jump ring to one cord end. Use the remaining 4mm jump ring to attach the antique brass clasp to the other cord end. Slide the pendant on the necklace.

Continued on page 18.

RED LEATHER NECKLACE, BRACELET & RING continued

To make the Bracelet:

1. Cut the desired bracelet length from the purse handle. Place one bracelet end in a ribbon crimp. Use the chain-nose pliers to gently squeeze the crimp over the bracelet end. Repeat with the remaining ribbon crimp on the other end.
2. Use needle and thread to sew 6 beads and the button to the bracelet, knotting the thread securely at the beginning and at the end.
3. Join the silver 7mm jump rings to create an extender chain. Use a silver 4mm jump ring to join the chain to one bracelet end. Thread a bead onto the head pin. Make a wrapped bead dangle, attaching the head pin to the chain.
4. Join a 4mm jump ring to the other end of the bracelet. Use the remaining 4mm jump ring to join the clasp to the jump ring.

To make the Ring:

1. Determine your ring size by sliding a ring that fits on the mandrel and noting the size. You will wrap the wire around the mandrel at the next larger size.
2. Cut a 20" wire length. Starting in the middle of the wire, wrap each wire end around the mandrel for a total of 6 wraps (at the larger size determined in Step 1).
3. Bend the ends away from the mandrel and slide on the chandelier piece.
4. Bend the wire back down toward the ring. Remove the ring from the mandrel and wrap the ends around the ring 3-4 times. Trim the excess wire and pinch the ends in with the chain-nose pliers.

BUTTERFLY TIN NECKLACE

Shown on page 21.

SHOPPING LIST

Supplies and Instructions are for the Butterfly Tin Necklace; see page 20 for information about the Dragonfly Tin Necklace.

- ☐ small mint tin
- ☐ 2 10mm red beads
- ☐ 2 8mm teal beads
- ☐ 2 8mm faceted beige beads
- ☐ 4mm teal bead
- ☐ 4mm antique copper ball bead
- ☐ 22" length of antique brass chain
- ☐ antique brass lobster clasp
- ☐ 6 4mm antique brass jump rings
- ☐ 7mm antique brass jump ring
- ☐ 10 8mm antique brass bead caps
- ☐ 2 $^{1}/_{2}$" antique copper hoops
- ☐ 4 antique brass eye pins
- ☐ 3 antique brass head pins
- ☐ 9mm antique copper jump ring
- ☐ Vintaj® Patina For All Metals (Victorian Gold, Antique Copper)
- ☐ Vintaj® Glaze Metal Sealer
- ☐ Ranger® mini ink blending tool and sponge applicators
- ☐ black and light rust archival ink pads
- ☐ Tim Holtz® Distress Inks (Vintage Photo, Wild Honey, Seedless Preserves, and Picked Raspberry)
- ☐ antique copper key charm
- ☐ Tim Holtz® Idea-ology™ philosophy tag
- ☐ butterfly and script lettering rubber stamps
- ☐ 2 word stickers
- ☐ water-based dimensional adhesive (we used Judikins Diamond Glaze™)
- ☐ découpage glue
- ☐ white cardstock scrap
- ☐ $^{1}/_{8}$" dia. metal hole punch
- ☐ small paintbrush
- ☐ old toothbrush
- ☐ blow dryer
- ☐ wax paper
- ☐ round-nose pliers
- ☐ chain-nose pliers (2 pair)
- ☐ wire cutters

Be sure to read the General Instructions on pages 30-32 before making your project.

To make the Necklace:

Necklace Finished Length: About 23", excluding pendant

1. For the pendant, gently fold up the hinges on the tin and separate the 2 pieces; decide which half you will use. Draw around the tin piece on cardstock. Cut out the shape and trim the edges until it fits inside the tin piece.
2. Dab the back and side edges of the tin with 2-3 coats of Victorian Gold Patina. Lightly dab Antique Copper Patina in small areas. Allow to dry. Seal the tin and allow to dry.
3. Working on wax paper, dab the blending tool on the Picked Raspberry ink pad 2-3 times. Starting off the cardstock shape and moving the blending tool in a circular motion, lightly touch the outer edges of the cardstock and work inward. Add touches of Wild Honey at the center. Layer on more Picked Raspberry around the outer edges. Add touches of Seedless Preserves to the left edge.
4. Dip the toothbrush in water and lightly sprinkle the cardstock surface. The water and ink will react with one another to change the appearance. Blow dry the cardstock.

Continued on page 20.

5. Stamp the script lettering with the light rust ink on the cardstock. Stamp the butterfly with the black ink. Add some "antiquing" to the outer edges with the Vintage Photo ink. Lightly "antique" the edges of 2 word stickers with Vintage Photo ink and adhere to the cardstock. Allow to dry.
6. Use the découpage glue to adhere the cardstock in the tin piece. Apply a thin coat of découpage glue to the cardstock to seal. Once dry, use the dimensional adhesive to glue a bead cap and the 4mm teal bead to the cardstock.
7. Punch holes in the tin sides at the bottom center and at the top of the tin (2 holes to attach the chain).
8. Thread a head pin through the bottom hole (from inside to the outside). Thread on a beige bead, a bead cap, a red bead, and the copper bead. Make a wrapped loop. Use the 9mm jump ring to attach the philosophy tag to the loop.
9. Make 2 teal bead connectors, a beige bead connector, and a red bead connector with bead caps surrounding each bead.
10. From the chain, cut:
    - a 5 1/4" length
    - a 5" length
    - two 1 1/2" lengths
    - a 1 1/4" length
    - two 1" lengths
    - a 1/2" length
11. For one side of the necklace, join a 1" and a 1 1/2" chain length with a teal bead connector. Join the remaining 1" chain length to the free end of the 1 1/2" chain length with the red bead connector. Use a 4mm jump ring to join an antique copper hoop to the free end of the 1" chain length. Use a 4mm jump ring to join the 5" chain length to the antique copper hoop. Use a 4mm jump ring to attach the key charm to the antique copper hoop and to join the clasp to the free end of the 5" chain length.
12. For the remaining side of the necklace, join the 1 1/4" and the 1/2" chain length with the beige bead connector. Use a 4mm jump ring to join the remaining antique copper hoop to the free end of the 1/2" chain length. Use a 4mm jump ring to join the remaining 1 1/2" chain length to the antique copper hoop. Join the free end of the 1 1/2" chain length and the 5 1/4" chain length with the remaining teal bead connector. Join a 7mm jump ring to the free end of the 5 1/4" chain length.
13. To join the chain end to the pendant, thread a head pin through a hole on the tin top (from inside to the outside). Make a wrapped loop, sliding one free chain end onto the loop before wrapping. Repeat to join the remaining chain end to the pendant.

It's easy to change the look of the Butterfly Tin Necklace; change the Patina colors to Verdigris, Jade, and Antique Copper for the tin back. Distress the cardstock with Mowed Lawn and add Broken China at the center, "antique" the edges with Vintage Photo. Stamp script lettering on the cardstock with black ink. Stamp (use black ink), cut out, and attach a dragonfly. Add a word or two and a Chinese coin charm. For the chain, just slide a ready-made ball chain necklace through the wrapped loops on the tin pendant top.

imagine
dream
INSPIRE
3197
peace

LEATHER TASSEL NECKLACE

SHOPPING LIST

- ☐ old "leather" purse to cut tassel from
- ☐ brass lamp coupling
- ☐ 3/4" brass lamp seating ring
- ☐ 14mm bead
- ☐ 5mm bead
- ☐ 19" length of antique brass chain
- ☐ 9mm antique copper jump ring
- ☐ 2 4mm antique brass jump rings
- ☐ antique brass square toggle clasp
- ☐ 18-gauge antique copper wire
- ☐ Vintaj® Glaze Metal Sealer
- ☐ small paintbrush
- ☐ craft glue
- ☐ round-nose pliers
- ☐ chain-nose pliers (2 pair)
- ☐ wire cutters

Be sure to read the General Instructions on pages 30-32 before making your project.

To make the Necklace:

Necklace Finished Length: About 20", excluding pendant

1. Seal the lamp coupling and seating ring with the metal sealer; allow to dry.
2. For the tassel, cut a 3" x 2" piece of the purse "leather." Stopping 3/4" from the top edge, cut 1/4" wide fringe ***(Fig. 1)***.

Fig. 1

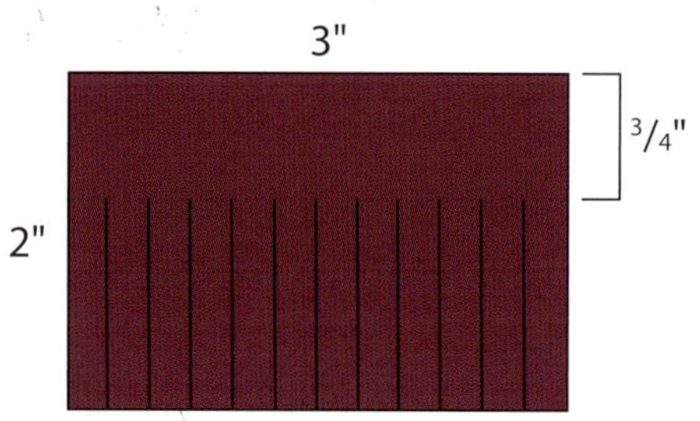

3. Tightly roll the tassel until it fits in the brass lamp coupling; trim any excess that does not fit in the lamp coupling. Glue the tassel in the lamp coupling.
4. Thread the 5mm bead on a 5" wire length. Secure the bead near one end by tightly wrapping the wire end around the longer section of the wire. Insert the wire through the tassel center ***(Fig. 2)***.

Fig. 2

5. Thread the 14mm bead on the wire and make a wrapped loop, adding the lamp seating ring before wrapping.
6. Attach the 9mm jump ring to the lamp seating ring and slide the tassel onto the chain. Use the 4mm jump rings to attach the clasp pieces to the chain ends.

NAUTICAL ANCHOR WASHER NECKLACE

SHOPPING LIST

- ☐ 1" washer
- ☐ scrap of chevron printed paper
- ☐ 24 seed beads to match paper
- ☐ silver anchor charm
- ☐ metal glue-on bail
- ☐ white wax linen cord
- ☐ 2 silver fold-over cord ends
- ☐ 4mm silver jump ring
- ☐ 7mm silver jump ring
- ☐ silver lobster clasp
- ☐ water-based dimensional adhesive (we used Judikins Diamond Glaze™)
- ☐ craft glue
- ☐ E-6000® industrial strength adhesive
- ☐ small paintbrush
- ☐ straight pin
- ☐ chain-nose pliers (2 pair)

Be sure to read the General Instructions on pages 30-32 before making your project.

Necklace Finished Length: About 20", excluding pendant

To make the Necklace:

1. To make the pendant, draw around the washer on the wrong side of the chevron paper; draw the inside circle too. Cut out the paper circle and the paper circle center. Use the dimensional adhesive to adhere the paper ring to the washer; let dry.
2. Apply a thick coat of dimensional adhesive to the paper surface; let dry. Apply a thin line of the dimensional adhesive to the back of the anchor charm; place the charm on the pendant and let dry.
3. Use E-6000 to glue the bail to the pendant back, trimming the bail length if necessary; let dry. Apply a coat of dimensional adhesive to the pendant back; let dry.
4. Cut a 30" length of cord. Tie an overhand knot about 4" from one cord end. Thread a seed bead on the cord and tie another overhand knot right next to the bead. Skip 2" and tie a knot; thread on a bead and tie another knot. Repeat twice more. Thread the pendant on the cord. Continue tying knots and adding beads until you have a total of 8 beads on the cord.
5. Repeat Step 4 twice so that you have 3 beaded cords.
6. Slide the beaded cords through the pendant so that the beads are offset from one another; trim the cords to 19" from end to end.
7. Attach a fold-over cord end to each set of cords.
8. Use the 4mm jump ring to attach the clasp to one cord end. Attach the 7mm jump ring to the remaining cord end.

BOTTLE CAP WATCH NECKLACE

SHOPPING LIST

- ☐ silver bottle cap
- ☐ old watch face to fit bottle cap
- ☐ 3/4" brass gear
- ☐ 65 3mm antique brass cube beads
- ☐ 8" length of antique silver large link chain
- ☐ 9" length of antique brass small link chain
- ☐ 22" length of 1.5mm brown leather cord
- ☐ 49-strand/.018 bead stringing wire
- ☐ 2 silver fold-over cord ends
- ☐ 2 silver crimp beads
- ☐ 4 7mm antique silver jump rings
- ☐ 5mm silver jump ring
- ☐ 2 4mm antique brass jump rings
- ☐ silver toggle clasp
- ☐ Tim Holtz® Idea-ology™ game spinner
- ☐ micro bolt, washer, and nut
- ☐ craft glue
- ☐ 1/8" dia. metal hole punch
- ☐ crimp tool
- ☐ chain-nose pliers (2 pair)
- ☐ wire cutters

Be sure to read the General Instructions *on pages 30-32* *before making your project.*

Necklace Finished Length: About 23"

To make the Necklace:

1. Cut the leather cord in half. Lay the cord lengths side by side and attach a fold-over cord end to each set of leather cord ends.
2. Punch a hole in the center of the bottle cap. Layer the watch face, gear, and game spinner in the bottle cap. Use the micro bolt assembly to secure the pieces in place.
3. Punch a hole at the top edge and the bottom edge of the bottle cap. Use a 7mm jump ring to join one end of the leather cord to the top hole. Use a 7mm jump ring to join the remaining leather cord end to the 5mm jump ring. Join the toggle bar to the 5mm jump ring.
4. Attach a 7mm jump ring to the bottom hole of the bottle cap; attach the remaining 7mm jump ring to the first jump ring. Use a crimp bead to join a 12" length of stringing wire to the this jump ring. Thread the cube beads on the wire. Use a crimp bead to attach the wire to the loop portion of the clasp.
5. Use a 4mm antique brass jump ring to join one end of the antique brass chain to the jump ring with the cube beaded strand. Use the remaining 4mm antique brass jump ring to join the remaining end of the antique brass chain to the loop portion of the clasp.
6. Join one end of the antique silver chain to the jump ring with the cube beaded strand and the antique brass chain. Join the remaining end of the antique silver chain to the loop portion of the clasp.

CORK SLICES BRACELET

SHOPPING LIST

- ☐ 2 wine corks (one with date or image on end)
- ☐ 2 buttons (one larger than the other)
- ☐ old watch face
- ☐ lock and key toggle clasp
- ☐ 7-9 5mm antique brass jump rings
- ☐ 1/2" length of medium link silver chain
- ☐ 10-14 7/16" steel screw eyes
- ☐ 1/2" brass gear
- ☐ 3/4" silver gear
- ☐ 3/8" silver washer
- ☐ 3/16" silver hex nut
- ☐ micro bolt with nut
- ☐ Tim Holtz® Idea-ology™ small game spinner
- ☐ E-6000® industrial strength adhesive
- ☐ black fine-point marker
- ☐ chain-nose pliers (2 pair)
- ☐ serrated blade craft saw
- ☐ 2" wide binder clip

Be sure to read the General Instructions on pages 30-32 before making your project.

To make the Bracelet:

1. Measure the clasp; add 1/2". Subtract this measurement from the desired bracelet length.
2. Use the marker to draw a line around a cork 1/4" from one end. Place the cork in the binder clip and align the drawn line with the edge of the binder clip. Hold the craft saw against the binder clip and cut a disk of cork ***(Fig. 1)***. Cut 5-7 cork disks.

Fig. 1

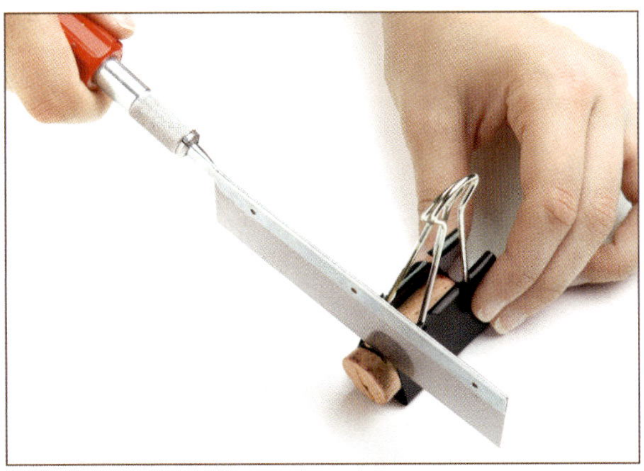

3. Decorate the cork disks as desired with the buttons, watch face, gears, washer, hex nut, micro bolt assembly, and game spinner, using E-6000 to adhere the pieces to the cork. If you have a printed cork disk, let the writing be the decorative element. Allow the adhesive to dry.
4. Twist a screw eye into either side of each cork disk, adding a drop of E-6000 as you twist in each eye. Once the adhesive is dry, join the disks with the jump rings until the bracelet is as close as possible to the length determined in Step 1.
5. Use a jump ring to attach the chain to one end of the bracelet; use a jump ring to attach the toggle bar to the chain. Use a jump ring to attaching the clasp loop to the remaining bracelet end.

SEIKO
SPIRIT

GENERAL INSTRUCTIONS

TOOLS

Chain-nose pliers have rounded, tapered jaws and a flat interior surface that will not mar wire. These pliers are used for reaching into tight places, gripping objects, opening and closing jump rings, and bending wire.

Round-nose pliers have round jaws that are useful for making loops and bending wire smoothly.

Wire cutters are used to cut small gauge wire, head pins, and eye pins.

A **crimp tool** (also known as crimping pliers) flattens and shapes the crimp bead or crimp tube.

Chain-nose pliers

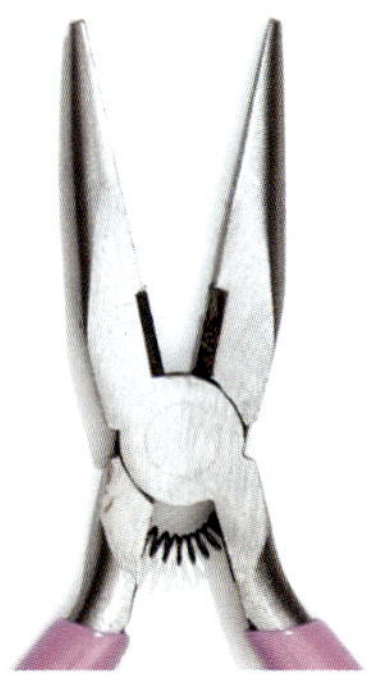

Round-nose pliers

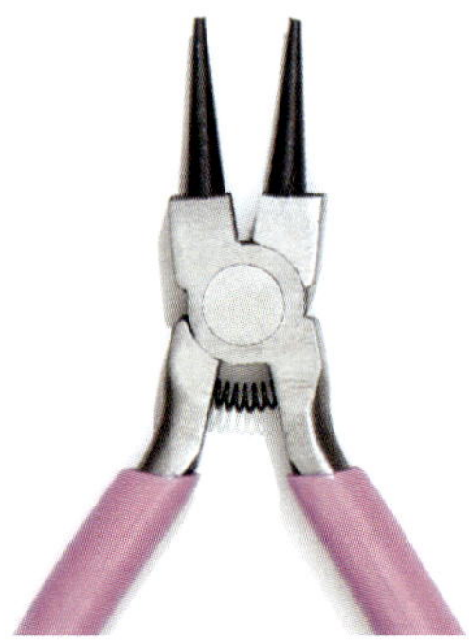

Wire cutters

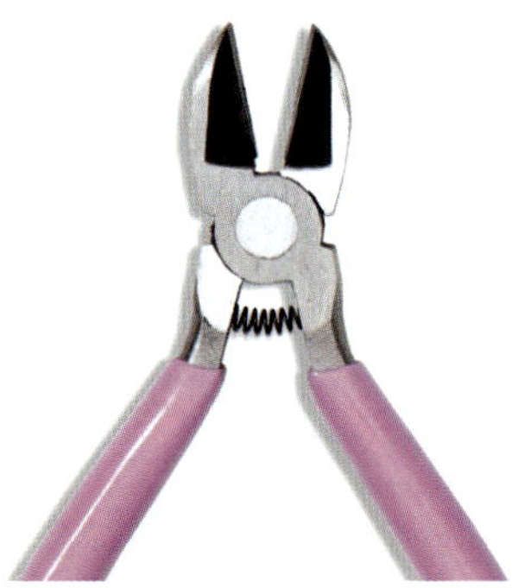

Crimp Tool

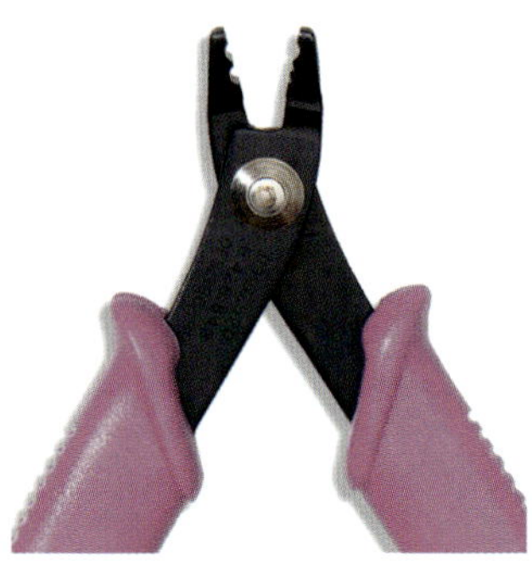

TECHNIQUES

Opening and Closing Loops, Chain Links, or Jump Rings

Hold one side of the loop, link, or jump ring with chain-nose pliers. With a second pair of chain-nose pliers, gently hold the other side of the loop. Open the loop by pulling one pair of pliers toward you while pushing the other away *(Fig. 1)*.

Close the loop by pushing and pulling the pliers in opposite directions, bringing the loop ends back together.

Making Bead Dangles and Bead Connectors

To make a bead dangle, slide the bead(s) on a head pin. Leaving about $^{1}/_{2}$", cut off the excess wire. Using chain-nose pliers, bend the wire at a 90° angle *(Fig. 2)*. Grasp the wire end with the round-nose pliers. Turn the pliers and bend the wire into a loop *(Figs. 3-4)*. Release the pliers. Straighten or twist the loop further if necessary.

To make a bead connector, slide the bead(s) on an eye pin. Follow bead dangle instructions, above, to make a loop on the end of an eye pin.

Fig. 1

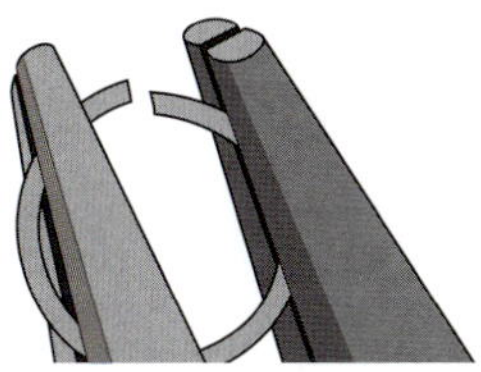

Fig. 2

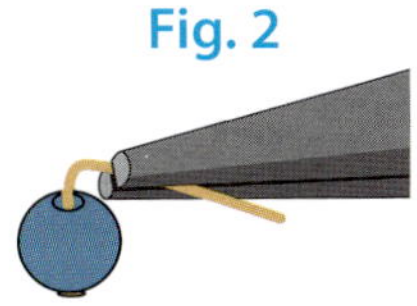

Fig. 3

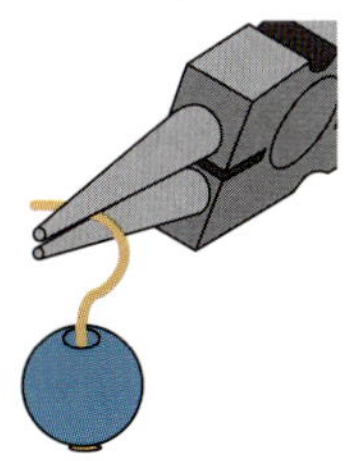

Fig. 4

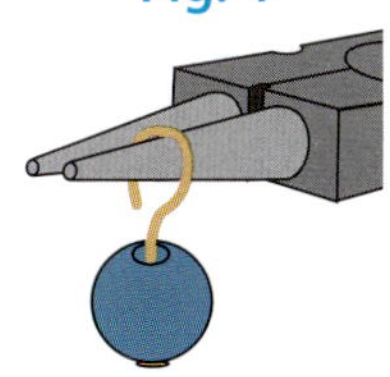

Making a Wrapped Loop on a Head Pin, Eye Pin, or Wire End

Slide the bead(s) on a head pin, eye pin, or wire end. Using chain-nose pliers, bend the wire at a 90° angle about $^{1}/_{8}$" above the bead *(Fig. 5)*. Grasp the wire with the round-nose pliers at the 90° bend. Use your finger to push the wire around the barrel of the pliers *(Fig. 6)*. Remove the pliers. Now is the time to slide the loop onto your project or to add something to the wrapped loop. Holding the loop with the chain-nose pliers, use a second pair of chain-nose pliers to wrap the wire end around itself above the bead 3-5 times *(Fig. 7)*. Trim the excess wire and tuck the wire end into the wraps with the chain-nose pliers.

Fig. 5

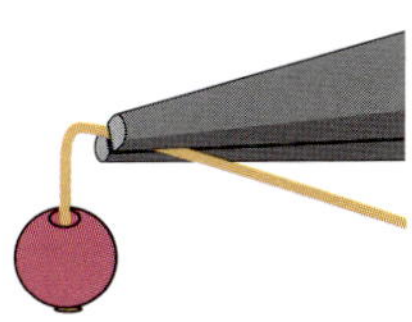

Fig. 6

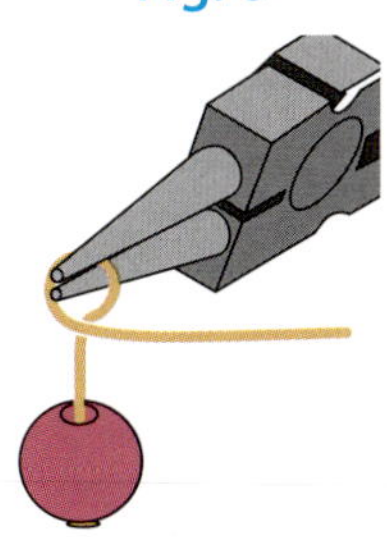

Fig. 7

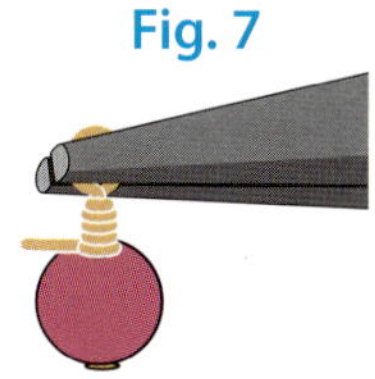

Using Crimp Beads

To finish a wire end, thread a crimp bead and the clasp or jump ring on the wire. Run the wire back through the crimp bead; use a pair of chain-nose pliers to pull and tighten the wire *(Fig. 8)*. Place the crimp bead on the inner groove of the crimp tool and squeeze *(Fig. 9)*.

Fig. 8

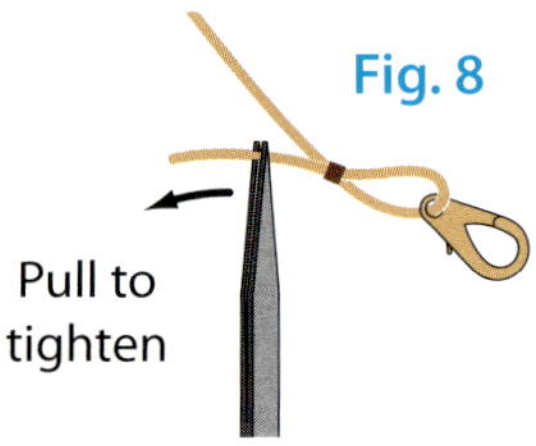

Fig. 9

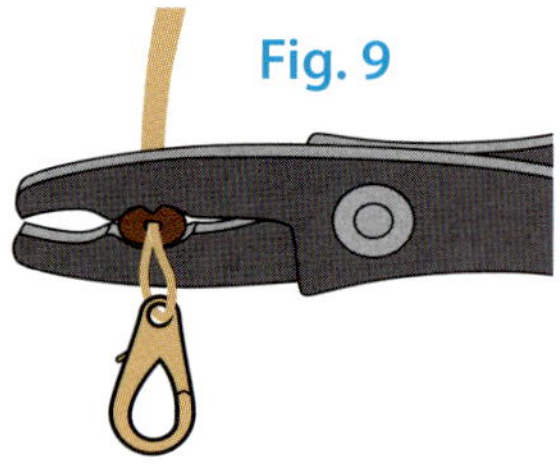

Release the tool, turn the crimp bead a quarter turn, and place it in the outer groove *(Fig. 10)*. Squeeze the tool to round out the crimp bead *(Fig. 11)*. Trim the wire end or if the design calls for beads, thread the beads over the wire to cover the end.

Fig. 10

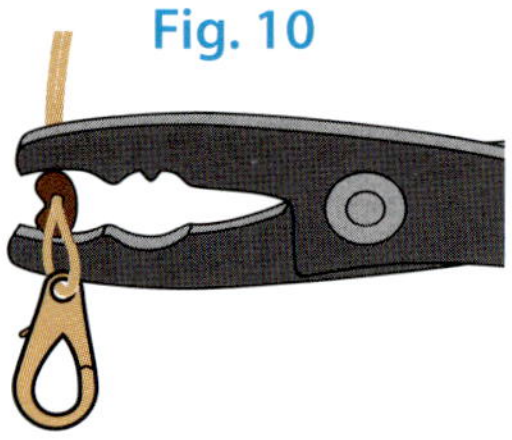

Fig. 11

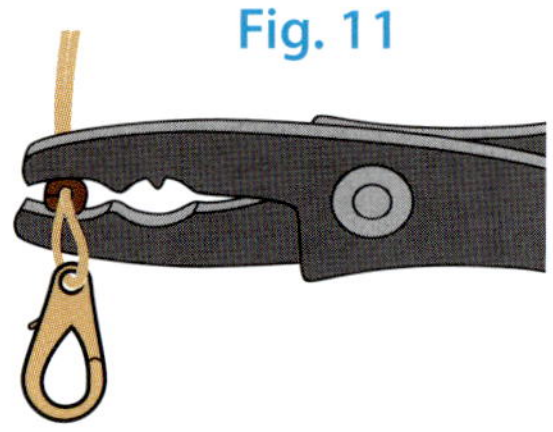

Tying Knots Between Beads

As you tie an overhand knot, slip a straight pin in the knot loop and guide the knot as close to the bead as possible *(Fig. 12)* near one end.

Fig. 12

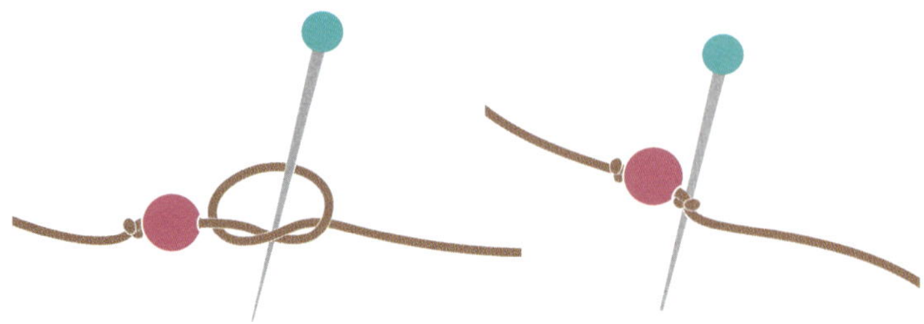

Attaching Fold-over Cord Ends

Place end(s) of the suede or cord in a fold-over cord end. Apply a drop of craft glue and use the chain-nose pliers to fold the ends over the suede or cord *(Fig. 13)*.

Fig. 13

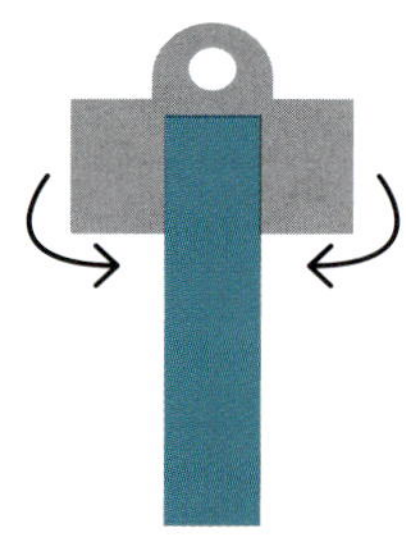

Holly Witt-Allen would like to thank Blue Moon Beads, Beaducation, Hip Chickee Beads (found on etsy.com), Beadalon, and Vintaj Natural Brass Co. for providing some of the products used for her jewelry designs.

Production Team: Technical Writer – Mary Sullivan Hutcheson; Technical Associate – Lisa Lancaster; Editorial Writer – Susan Frantz Wiles; Senior Graphic Artist – Lora Puls; Graphic Artist – Cailen Cochran; Photostylist – Lori Wenger; Photographer – Jason Masters.